This book is dedicated to you.

You are seen, you are known, you are loved.

You are enough.

ISBN 978-0-9992773-2-4

Scripture quotations are from New Revised Standard Version Bible: Catholic Edition, copyright © 1989, 1993 National Council of the Churches of Christ in the United States of America. Used by permission. All rights reserved.

www.creatingtolove.com

PSALM ONE HUNDRED THIRTY-NINE

Mary Williams

2018

TABLE OF CONTENTS

7   About Ruah

8   About the Artwork

9   How To Use This Book

13   Rest

17   Read

31   Remain

59   Renew

63   Record

100   Connect

RUAH
[ROO - ah]
noun

a Hebrew word meaning
breath or Spirit

ABOUT RUAH

Day by day. Hour by hour.
Even minute by minute.
Every breath we take can be offered as prayer.

The Ruah series encourages everyday faithful to
encounter well-known Scripture passages and prayers with
deeper intentionality and mindfulness. It is in quiet,
purposeful prayer that we come to know and
be known more fully by God.

May this book give you the opportunity
to be still, to meditate, and to contemplate.

May this book open your heart to new ways of
understanding God's deep and unabiding love for you.

May this book encourage you to breathe in the Spirit.

God's gift of ruah is yours.

ABOUT THE ARTWORK

The medium used for the cover artwork of the Ruah series is alcohol ink. A final piece is created by using one's breath to move this highly-pigmented, fast-drying ink around synthetic paper.

Alcohol ink is beautifully unpredictable. You never quite know how it will look when it dries. You can manipulate the ink only in as much as your breath gives it movement. In the same way that the artist gives life to the alcohol ink through her breath, God gives life to us through His gift of ruah. God's life-giving breath fills our souls with joy, peace, and hope.

Occasionally, you will see three lines flowing through the pages of this book. The lines mimic the drying marks of the alcohol ink, but more significantly, they represent the Father, Son, and Holy Spirit breathing life into you as you pray.

HOW TO USE THIS BOOK

Each Ruah book is divided into five sections loosely inspired by the Catholic tradition of *lectio divina*:

REST | an opportunity to be still and silent before beginning your time in prayer

READ | a slow and intentional reading of the prayer

REMAIN | another reading of the prayer in which you'll find added reflection questions to encourage you to encounter the prayer more deeply in conversation with God

RENEW | additional questions to further ponder new observations in your heart as you finish this prayerful experience

RECORD | a perpetual journal for you to write down any insights you'd like to remember. The perpetual journal can be used as often or as little as you choose during each reading

Use the various sections of this book based on your own unique needs as the Spirit moves in and through you.

PSALM ONE HUNDRED THIRTY-NINE

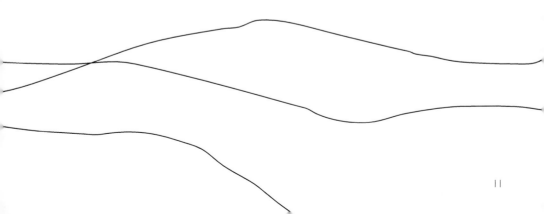

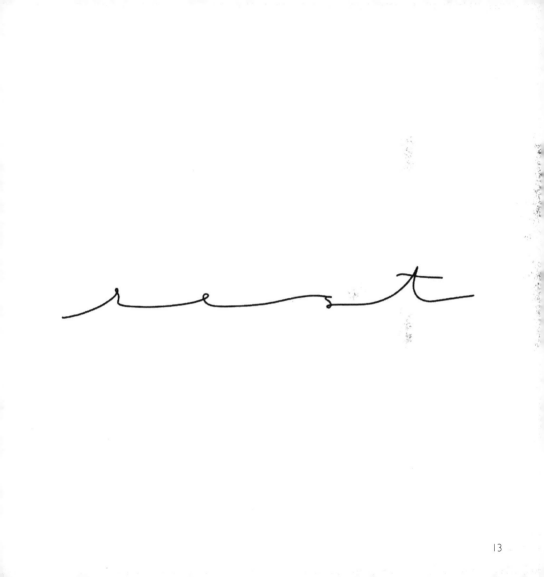

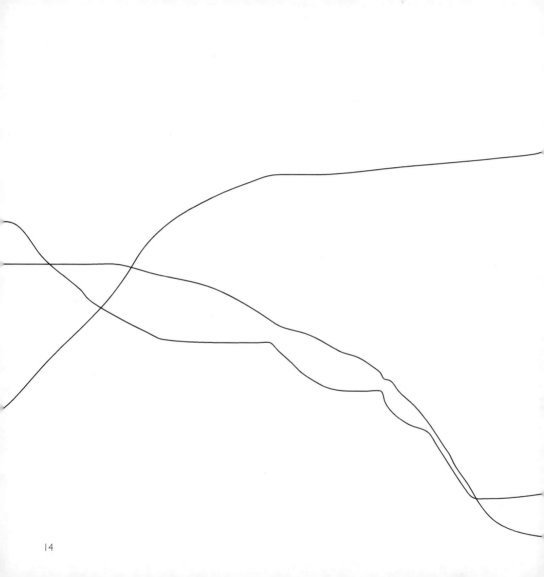

Take a moment
to be still,
to be quiet,
to enter into prayer.
Breathe.

read

O Lord, you have searched me and know me.

You know when I sit down and when I rise up;

you discern my thoughts from far away.

You search out my path and my lying down,

and are acquainted with all my ways.

Even before a word is on my tongue,

O Lord, you know it completely.

You hem me in, behind and before,
and lay your hand upon me.
Such knowledge is too wonderful for me;
it is so high that I cannot attain it.

Where can I go from your spirit?
Or where can I flee from your presence?
If ascend to heaven, you are there;
if I make my bed in Sheol, you are there.

If I take the wings of the morning
and settle at the farthest limits of the sea,
even there your hand shall lead me,
and your right hand shall hold me fast.

If I say, "Surely the darkness shall cover me,
and the light around me become night,"
even the darkness is not dark to you;
the night is as bright as the day,
for darkness is as light to you.

For it was you who formed my inward parts;

you knit me together in my mother's womb.

I praise you, for I am fearfully and wonderfully made.

Wonderful are your works;

that I know very well.

My frame was not hidden from you,

when I was being made in secret,

intricately woven in the depths of the earth.

Your eyes beheld my unformed substance.

In your book were written all the days that were formed for me,

when none of them as yet existed.

How weighty to me are your thoughts, O God!

How vast is the sum of them!

I tried to count them - they are more than the sand;

I come to the end - I am still with you.

O that you would kill the wicked, O God,
and that the bloodthirsty would depart from me -
those who speak of you maliciously,
and lift themselves up against you for evil!

Do I not hate those who hate you, O Lord?

And do I not loathe those who rise up against you?

I hate them with perfect hatred;

I count them my enemies.

Search me, O God, and know my heart;

test me and know my thoughts.

See if there is any wicked way in me,

and lead me in the way everlasting.

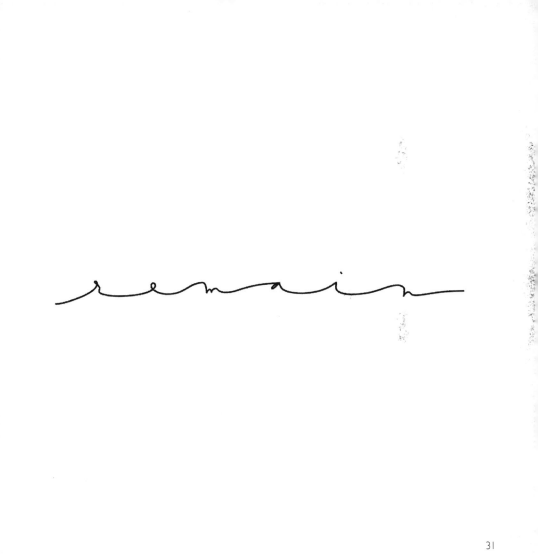

As you read Psalm 139 again on the left hand pages,
take time to ponder the Spirit moving through you
as you talk to God using the reflection questions
on the right hand pages.

O Lord, you have searched me and know me.

You know when I sit down and when I rise up;

you discern my thoughts from far away.

What thoughts and prayers
are present in my heart today?

Do I believe that you already
know and understand them, God?

Am I ready to share them
openly with you?

You search out my path and my lying down,
and are acquainted with all my ways.
Even before a word is on my tongue,
O Lord, you know it completely.

*What does it feel like to really
believe that you are familiar with
all the parts, both good and bad,
of my life?*

You hem me in, behind and before,

and lay your hand upon me.

Such knowledge is too wonderful for me;

it is so high that I cannot attain it.

When I ponder your wonderful
presence, God,
what comes to my mind?

When I think about you,
these are the questions that
I would like to ask you.

Where can I go from your spirit?
Or where can I flee from your presence?
If ascend to heaven, you are there;
if I make my bed in Sheol, you are there.

*What does it feel like to know
that you are always with me, God?*

*What are moments in which I
feel close to you?
What are moments in which I feel
distant from you?*

If I take the wings of the morning
and settle at the farthest limits of the sea,
even there your hand shall lead me,
and your right hand shall hold me fast.

*What experiences happening
in my life right now make me desire
your comforting guidance?*

*In what ways might I be
trying to wander from your love?*

If I say, "Surely the darkness shall cover me,
and the light around me become night,"
even the darkness is not dark to you;
the night is as bright as the day,
for darkness is as light to you.

What are the light and
dark places of my life?

Are there areas of my life that
especially need illuminating?
What are they?

For it was you who formed my inward parts;

you knit me together in my mother's womb.

I praise you, for I am fearfully and wonderfully made.

Wonderful are your works;

that I know very well.

What does it feel like to be
known and loved
so intimately by you, God?

Do I truly believe that
I am wonderfully made?

How might I praise you today?

My frame was not hidden from you,

when I was being made in secret,

intricately woven in the depths of the earth.

Your eyes beheld my unformed substance.

In your book were written all the days that were formed for me,

when none of them as yet existed.

Do I believe that there are
wonderful things planned
for my life? Why or why not?

What goals or dreams do I have
right now that I feel are
a gift from you?

Where do I feel I need to share
my gifts tomorrow...
next year...in ten years?

How weighty to me are your thoughts, O God!

How vast is the sum of them!

I tried to count them - they are more than the sand;

I come to the end - I am still with you.

*What are some of the blessings
in my life? Does it feel easy or
challenging to name them? Why?*

*Where in my daily routine
do I see you, God?*

*Where do I see you
in the world around me?*

O that you would kill the wicked, O God,
and that the bloodthirsty would depart from me -
those who speak of you maliciously,
and lift themselves up against you for evil!

*Are there unhealthy parts of
my life that need destroying?
What are they?*

*How are these taking away
from my relationship with you?*

Do I not hate those who hate you, O Lord?
And do I not loathe those who rise up against you?
I hate them with perfect hatred;
I count them my enemies.

*As I call to mind someone that
I consider an enemy,
I ponder how I might be able
to love them into you instead.*

*As I call to mind something
in my life that I hate,
I ponder how I might be able
to overcome it with love?*

Search me, O God, and know my heart;

test me and know my thoughts.

See if there is any wicked way in me,

and lead me in the way everlasting.

*In what ways, God,
do I long for you to encouage
or challenge me to share my gifts,
to love others, and
to live out my vocation?*

*How is my life and
my world-view changed
by knowing I am so loved by you?*

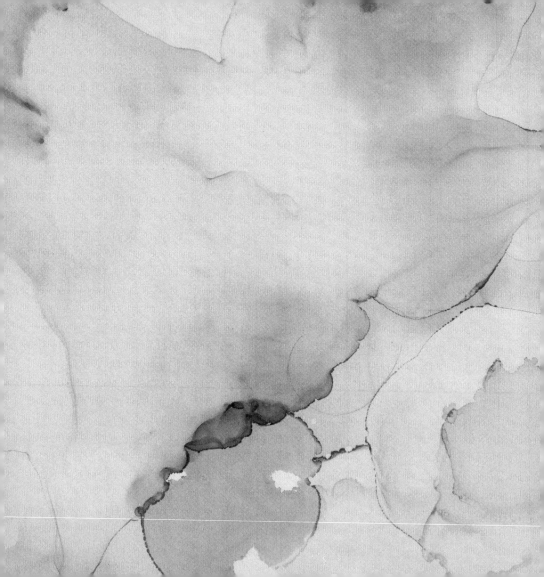

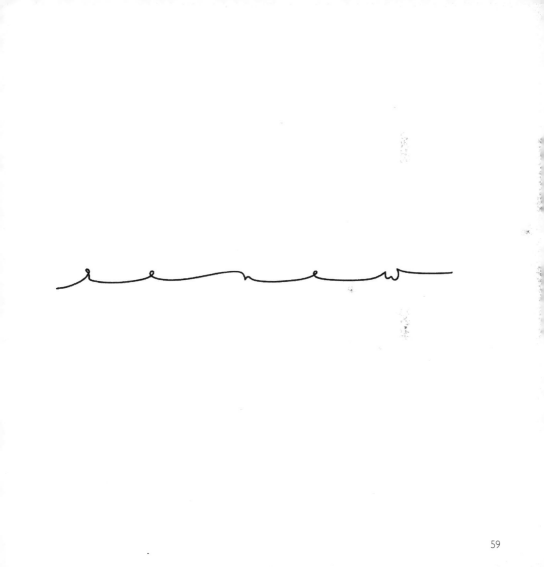

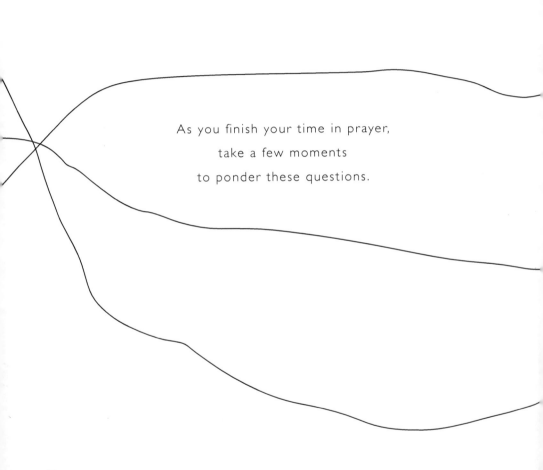

As you finish your time in prayer,
take a few moments
to ponder these questions.

In what ways has this prayer
transformed my heart today?

Has praying Psalm 139 called me
to action of any kind?
What is it and what steps
will I take to make it happen?

As I enter back in my daily routine,
in what ways do I feel renewed
in my relationship with God?

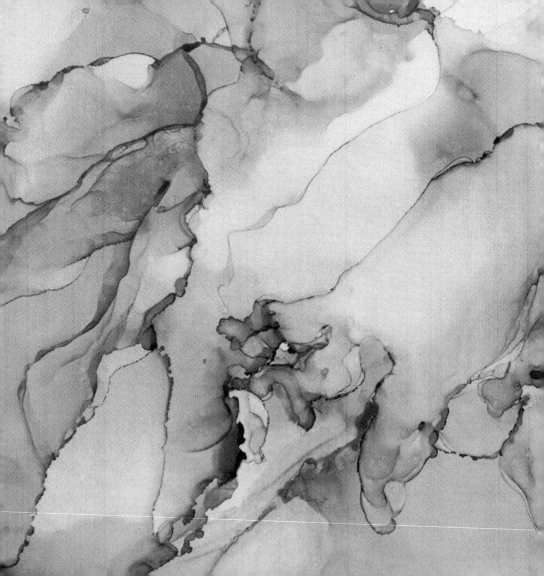

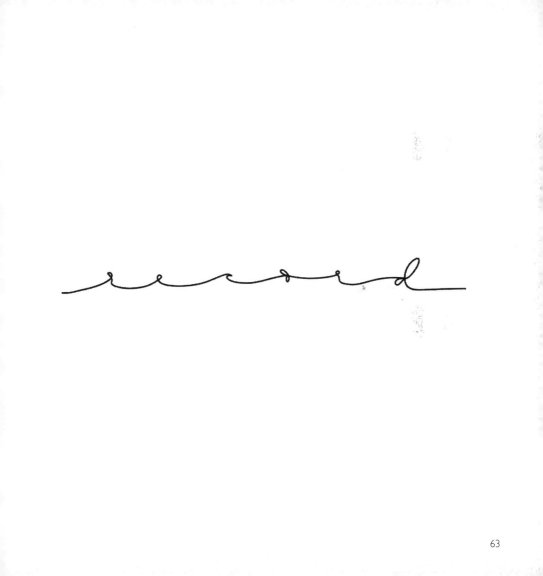

Please use this perpetual journal
as a place to record any heartful insights
you'd like to remember or revisit.

SEARCH ME, O GOD,
AND KNOW MY *heart*

YOU knit

ME TOGETHER IN
MY MOTHER'S WOMB

I PRAISE YOU
BECAUSE I AM
FEARFULLY AND

wonderfully

MADE

LEAD ME
IN THE WAY

everlasting

CONNECT
www.creatingtolove.com
Instagram @creatingtolove
facebook.com/creatingtolove
#ruahbooks

94063000R00057

Made in the USA
Columbia, SC
18 April 2018